The Pressed Flower

Project Book

Joanna Sheen

MEREHURST

Published in 1993 by Merehurst Limited
Ferry House, 51-57 Lacy Road, Putney, London SW15 1PR
Text © copyright Joanna Sheen 1993
Photographs © copyright Merehurst Limited 1993

Reprinted 1993, 1995 (twice)

ISBN 1-85391-208-5

A catalogue record for this book is available from the British Library.

Managing Editor **Heather Dewhurst**
Edited by **Diana Brinton**
Designed by **Lisa Tai**
Photography by **Debbie Patterson** (cover, and pages 4-5, 8-9, 13, 14-15, 18-19,
22-3, 27, 30-31, 36-7, 42-3, 47); all other photography by **Mike Evans**.
Typesetting by **Litho Link Limited**
Colour separation by **Fotographics Ltd UK - Hong Kong**
Printed in Italy by **G Canale & C SpA**

*Merehurst is a leading publisher of craft books and has an excellent range of titles
to suit all levels. Please send to the address above for our free catalogue, stating
the title of this book.*

Contents

Introduction

The craft of pressing flowers is a wonderfully relaxing hobby that can bring a new dimension to country walks and give an added bonus to gardening and even to growing plants in a window box. Although it is very useful to have a large garden in which to grow suitable plants for pressing, you can also press flowers and leaves picked from friends' gardens or – if you are in the middle of a city and have no other options – you will discover that your local florist may have many suitable subjects for pressing.

There are many small projects you can make from the very beginning and, with a little practice, all the projects in this book are within the capabilities of a fairly new pressed flower enthusiast. Flowers fall into different colour groups and the foliage into shapes and sizes, and as you collect a variety of both, ideas for pictures should spring to mind.

Pressed flower basics

You need only a minimum amount of equipment to press flowers successfully. The first item is a flower press. Although you can use old books, there are many small flowers and leaves that are best treated in a traditional press. Since presses are very simple to make and cheap to buy it is preferable to use one to start with.

If you do not wish to use a traditional flower press, telephone directories, which have absorbent pages, offer a practical alternative. You will need to put further books or other weights on top of the directory in order to give some pressure.

Most pressed flower pictures can be made with a standard craft glue, which is a latex adhesive. This rubs off if you spill some on the card on which you are laying your flowers, but it may leave a mark. It holds the flowers well, however, and does not produce any brown marks on the pressed materials, or at least not for some time.

PRESSING

If your press is a purchased model, begin by discarding the corrugated cardboard inside the press – the cardboard tends to leave unsightly lines across the pressed flowers. Start with a layer of newspaper, then cover this with a sheet of blotting paper. Lay the flowers on the blotting paper, making sure that none of them overlap and all are well within the edges of the blotting paper. Cover the flowers with another layer of blotting paper and then more newspaper. The next layer starts with another sheet of blotting paper, and you can continue until you have ten layers of flowers in the press. Cover this last layer with blotting paper and then newspaper, and screw the press down as firmly as possible.

Label your press clearly, listing the contents and the date on which they went into the press. It is also useful to add where you picked the flowers. Otherwise you may find, when you open the press and are delighted with its contents, that you have no idea where the flowers came from.

Put the labelled press in a warm place – preferably an airing cupboard – where the temperature will remain fairly constant. Leave it for between six and eight weeks, by which time the flowers will be dried and pressed. Resist the temptation to open the press too early in order to look and see how things are progressing; pressed flowers are very delicate while they are drying, and you may damage them.

If you are using a telephone directory instead of a press, place the flowers or leaves between sheets of blotting paper. Several books with blotting paper folders inside can be piled up. It is still, of course, important to label them just as you would label a press.

STORAGE AND PROTECTION

Once the flowers are ready, you can remove them from the press and keep them in clear-fronted paper bags. Never store pressed flowers in polythene bags as they will sweat and go mouldy.

Pressed flower pictures should always be hung out of the light – bright light will cause the colour in the flowers and leaves to fade. However, a picture made with pressed materials that have been chosen for their good quality and their colour retention can be hung in a shady place and will continue to look attractive for many years. There are pictures that are six years old in my house, and they still look as good as new, but I do live in a very old cottage, with small windows that restrict the amount of light to which the pictures are subjected.

CHOOSING YOUR MATERIALS

Many flowers and leaves are suitable for pressing, but those that are naturally flatter are much easier to press than multi-petalled varieties, such as carnations or tea roses. If you want to press one of the latter, then it must be taken to pieces petal by petal, pressed, and then reassembled when used in a picture.

Some flowers keep their colour dramatically better than others, and this can be discovered by trial and error from among the flowers available to each individual. As a rough guideline, pale pinks and peach tones can be very difficult to retain, whereas oranges and autumnal shades tend to be strong and last for a long time. A good way to test the colourfast properties of a plant is to press a selection of flowers taken from it; place these under glass on a sunny windowsill for a couple of weeks, and see what happens. Keep notes, and press more of those materials that keep their colour well, avoiding anything that fades too quickly.

Blue delphiniums and all the larkspur family make excellent subjects for pressing, as do most grey and silvery leaves. Ignore succulents, as these contain too much water, and avoid flowers that have particularly thick centres, such as large daisies or chrysanthemums.

Very little equipment is required, but a flower press is a useful investment.

Greetings card
&
Gift tag

A card made by the sender is a delightful way of marking a special occasion, and with a little extra thought you can make a gift tag to match. On the following pages are two different design ideas.

Greetings card

A design for a card can be as straightforward or as complex as you choose. Even the simplest of cards, perhaps made with just a single flower and a couple of leaves, can look most attractive and will be kept long after a purchased card would have been thrown away. Prepared blanks are available from various sources, including some stationers, art shops and craft suppliers. If you wish to make a matching tag, following the method overleaf, you might use one red rose backed with small raspberry leaves.

INGREDIENTS

Card blank (see page 48 for suppliers)

❧

Clear film, of the type used to cover books

❧

A selection of flowers and leaves

❧

Latex adhesive

1 Lay the card on a clean surface. Using tweezers, carefully position the leaves to be used in your chosen design. This arrangement was made with a combination of blackberry leaves and Artemisia 'Lambrook Silver'.

2 *Add your chosen flowers, ensuring that they do not overlap leaves or stalks to any great extent. If necessary, you can trim away excess leaves and stalks that would otherwise underlie the flowers, creating ridges and lumps that might spoil the design. The flowers used for this particular design were roses and pink larkspur.*

3 *Using a large tapestry needle, carefully apply a little latex glue underneath each leaf and flower. When you have completed the picture and are happy with it, cut a sufficiently large rectangle of the clear film to cover the design area. Peel away the backing and then, starting from one corner, carefully lay the film over the design. The best film to use is the type that can be treated with an iron to give a better finish. Lay a piece of thin foam over the design and, with the iron on a cool setting, press firmly for about 30 seconds and then check that the result is perfect.*

ift tag

Gift tags are easy to make and offer an ideal way of introducing children to pressed flower work. The same basic method can also be used to make a bookmark, which would be a delightful and treasured gift for a much-loved grandparent. You can purchase gift card blanks or make your own from thin card. A tip if you are making your own card is to cut the card about 12mm (½in) larger than the finished size and then, when the design is finished and protected with film, fold the card and trim it to size with a craft knife and metal ruler.

INGREDIENTS

Thin card or purchased gift card blank

ઝ

Thin crochet cotton or wool, for a tie

ઝ

Clear film, of the type used to cover books

ઝ

A selection of flowers and leaves

ઝ

Latex adhesive

Place the card on a flat surface. Start by positioning leaves, in this case raspberry leaves, then add one or two small flowers, such as the forget-me-not sprays shown here. Finish by covering with clear film and ironing it in place, as for the card on the previous page.

Family album

This photograph frame, with its host of small family pictures, would make an excellent gift for a grandparent, although you might be tempted to keep it for yourself.

$\mathcal{F}$amily album

You will need to select fairly small flowers and leaves for this project, as the space available between the apertures is somewhat limited. You may be able to find a mount of this general type in stock at your local picture framer, or if not he should be able to prepare one for you (in which case you could specify a slightly more generous spacing). A fairly subtle scheme is often more successful than a very bright collection of flowers, as the latter tend to overshadow the photographs displayed.

INGREDIENTS

30cm × 25cm (12in × 10in) frame, with glass cut to fit and a hardboard back

❧

Mount to fit, with several apertures

❧

Family photographs

❧

A selection of small flowers and leaves

❧

Latex adhesive

❧

Masking tape

1 Start by assembling all the elements and considering the relationships of colour and scale. Bear in mind that the space between the apertures is small and large leaves or flowers would also look out of proportion with the pictures.

2 *Choose small leaves, like the blackberry leaves used here. Lay them in position on the card, allowing them to overlap the holes slightly, if necessary.*

3 *Add some flowers to the design. This one was made with peach potentillas and 'Ballerina' roses. You might select your flowers for their sentimental associations or to blend with the decor of the album's intended setting.*

4 *Finish with some smaller flowers and delicate bits and pieces to add a dainty feel to the design – lawn daisies, small pieces of elderflower and melilot (yellow clover) were added here. Using a large needle and latex adhesive, secure each separate item in place. The photographs can be fixed to the back of the mount with masking tape. Cover the finished mount with the (cleaned) glass, and insert both into the frame.*

Wedding photograph frame

This would make a delightful gift for a friend or relative as a memento of a wedding or anniversary, or you might use it as a frame for a very special photograph of your own.

Wedding photograph frame

This particular design was created from flowers taken from a bride's bouquet, to add a personal and extra-romantic touch to the finished frame. Where a bride has chosen a white arrangement you could follow the Victorian example and use flower language to express the theme. Try using red rose petals for love with forget-me-nots for faithfulness, for example, as a backing for a selection of the white flowers from the bouquet. Choose a mount that has a single aperture offset, to leave plenty of space for your design.

INGREDIENTS

35cm × 30cm (14in × 12in) frame, with glass cut to measure and a hardboard back

A mount with an offset aperture

A selection of flowers, ferns and leaves

Latex adhesive

1 Lay the mount on a clean surface and arrange some materials – in this case asparagus fern, ivy leaves and gypsophila – around the aperture, allowing them to stray a little over the edge where appropriate, to soften the photograph.

2 *When the background foliage is in place, add the main flowers that will dominate the design, in this case some beautiful 'Minuet' roses. Make sure they are balanced so that the design does not look top heavy or so large as to overwhelm the photograph.*

3 *Finally, position the remaining elements of the design, in this case carnations and Singapore orchids, together with some additional small ivy leaves to give a little finishing touch. Using a large needle and the latex adhesive, glue the component parts of the arrangement firmly to the card. The photograph can then be taped in placed at the back of the mount (trim it, if necessary). Give the glass a final clean to make sure there are no smears or dust, then insert the completed mount into the frame.*

Spring

Creating a series of pictures to depict the seasons can offer a way of setting yourself an enjoyable challenge as you search for flowers and leaves appropriate to the period that you have in mind.

$\mathscr{S}$pring

Many spring flowers are more fragile than those pressed later in the year, so take extra care when assembling this picture. Another feature of spring flowers is that they tend to be a little translucent, so counteract this by using several, one on top of another, to create stronger colour. Scale also has to be borne in mind – full-size daffodils would completely overwhelm the tiny snowdrops, but the newer miniature varieties are ideal, and can be pressed face-up or sideways.

INGREDIENTS

30cm × 25cm (12in × 10in) frame

‰

A mount with an oval aperture

‰

Cream silk, slightly smaller than the mount

‰

27.5cm × 22.5cm (11in × 9in) of foam, 12mm (½in) thick

‰

Narrow masking tape

‰

Spring flowers and leaves

‰

Latex adhesive

1 Stretch the silk across the back of the mount and secure with masking tape. Make sure that the silk is taut, and free from wrinkles. Place the hardboard on a clean surface, smooth side up, and lay the foam over it and the prepared mount over both.

2 Lay the leaves in position. This design used a mixture of small rose leaves and ferns.

24

3 Continue to build the design, adding more leaves, clustered on a focal point, together with primroses and snowdrops. The primroses can be placed one on top of another to create a greater depth of colour.

4 Finally, add some more substantial flowers. This design incorporated Alchemilla mollis *leaves with small narcissi and touches of forget-me-not. Using a large needle, glue each piece in place with a little latex adhesive. Carefully clean the glass and place it on top of the picture. Place the frame in position and then turn the entire assembly upside down. The back can be secured with small panel pins placed at 2.5cm (1in) intervals, or with staples (use a framer's staple gun). Seal the back with masking tape.*

THE FOUR SEASONS

Summer

Summer is the easiest time in which to find suitable subjects for pressing – indeed, you may find that you are spoiled for choice, but this is a pleasurable problem to face on an autumn evening, as you pick and choose from the summer's offerings.

$\mathcal{S}$ummer

I have used single roses for this design as they are far easier to press and seem to keep their colour well. If you prefer to use hybrid tea roses, pick a newly-opened flower; strip the leaves and condition the stem by crushing it; place the rose in fairly deep water, and press just the outer petals at first, continuing to take the outer petals over two or three days as the flower opens fully. Do not press too heavily or the petals will lose their colour.

INGREDIENTS

30cm × 25cm (12in × 10in) frame

A mount with an oval aperture

Cream silk, slightly smaller than the mount

27.5cm × 22.5cm (11in × 9in) of foam, 12mm (¹⁄₂in) thick

Narrow masking tape

Summer flowers and leaves

Latex adhesive

1 *Prepare the mount and lay it over the hardboard and foam, as for the Spring picture (see step 1, page 24). Put spires of larkspur in the centre of the design; add two fairly large roses, and then tuck a couple of love-in-a-mist* (Nigella damascena) *between them.*

2 Add some leaves – this example was made with maidenhair fern and chamomile leaves. Position some individual flowers of pink larkspur to mingle with all the other flowers at the centre of the design, which should now be filling out attractively while retaining the strong focus of the roses.

3 Finish with chamomile daisies and buttercups, including buds as well as flowers. Fix the flowers and leaves in position, applying a little latex adhesive to the back of each with a large needle. Carefully clean the glass and place it on top of the picture. Place the frame in position and then turn the entire assembly upside down. The back can be secured with small panel pins placed at 2.5cm (1in) intervals, or with staples (use a framer's staple gun). Seal the back with masking tape.

Autumn & Winter

It is not so simple to find autumn or winter flowers and leaves that are
suitable for pressing, but this only adds to the excitement of the chase,
as you track down some new possibility.

utumn

Autumn leaves are among the easiest materials to press, and even very young children can handle them as they are tough and durable. If necessary, autumn leaves can even be pressed by ironing them for a couple of minutes between two sheets of blotting paper, with the iron on a medium hot setting. Artistic licence is permissible when you are creating seasonal pictures, and it is for you to decide how strictly you are going to keep to the theme.

INGREDIENTS

30cm × 25cm (12in × 10in) frame

❧

A mount with an oval aperture

❧

Cream silk, slightly smaller than the mount

❧

27.5cm × 22.5cm (11in × 9in) of foam, 12mm (½in) thick

❧

Narrow masking tape

❧

Autumn flowers and leaves

❧

Latex adhesive

1 Prepare the mount and lay it over the hardboard and foam, as for the Spring picture (see step 1, page 24). Begin the design with some autumnal leaves – in this case, maple leaves – of a suitable golden-brown variety.

2 Add the largest flowers in the design, which will essentially be a horseshoe shape. Red and yellow roses were used here. These may not be thought of as strictly autumn flowers, but some varieties have their second flowering well into the autumn, so a little artistic licence is permissible.

3 Add the other small components of the design, in this case some primulas (also not truly autumnal), some montbretia and some peach-coloured potentillas. Check the design from all angles, making sure that you have a balanced and pleasing combination. Fix the flowers and leaves in position, applying a little latex adhesive to the back of each with a large needle. Carefully clean the glass and place it on top of the picture.

inter

Winter may appear to be a difficult time to collect bits and pieces for pressing, but in fact some evergreens can be pressed, and there are several flowering shrubs and plants, such as heather, that can still be picked. Make sure that your findings are dry when you put them in the press. Be experimental in your hunt for materials: lichens, mosses and skeletonized leaves are all worth pressing, and you can spray dull-coloured items with gold paint for Christmas projects.

INGREDIENTS

30cm × 25cm (12in × 10in) frame

ꙮ

A mount with an oval aperture

ꙮ

Cream silk, slightly smaller than the mount

ꙮ

27.5cm × 22.5cm (11in × 9in) of foam, 12mm (¹/₂in) thick

ꙮ

Narrow masking tape

ꙮ

Wintery flowers and leaves

ꙮ

Latex adhesive

1 Prepare the mount and lay it over the hardboard and foam, as for the Spring picture (see step 1, page 24). Begin by establishing the leafy background; a mixture of conifer and ivy with bright red late-autumn leaves was used here.

2 Add some strong, Christmas-red roses to the centre of the design. The rose used here is a single-flowered variety called 'Robin Redbreast' – it may not be quite in season but at least the name is appropriate to the theme! Red and green bracts of euphorbia (sometimes called spurge) were also added at this stage.

3 Fill out the design with pieces of grey artemisia, heather, tiny pieces of blossom and dark red rose buds. Fix the flowers and leaves in position, applying a little latex adhesive to the back of each with a large needle. Carefully clean the glass and place it on top of the picture. Place the frame in position and then turn the entire assembly upside down. The back can be secured with small panel pins placed at 2.5cm (1in) intervals, or with staples (use a framer's staple gun). Seal the back with masking tape.

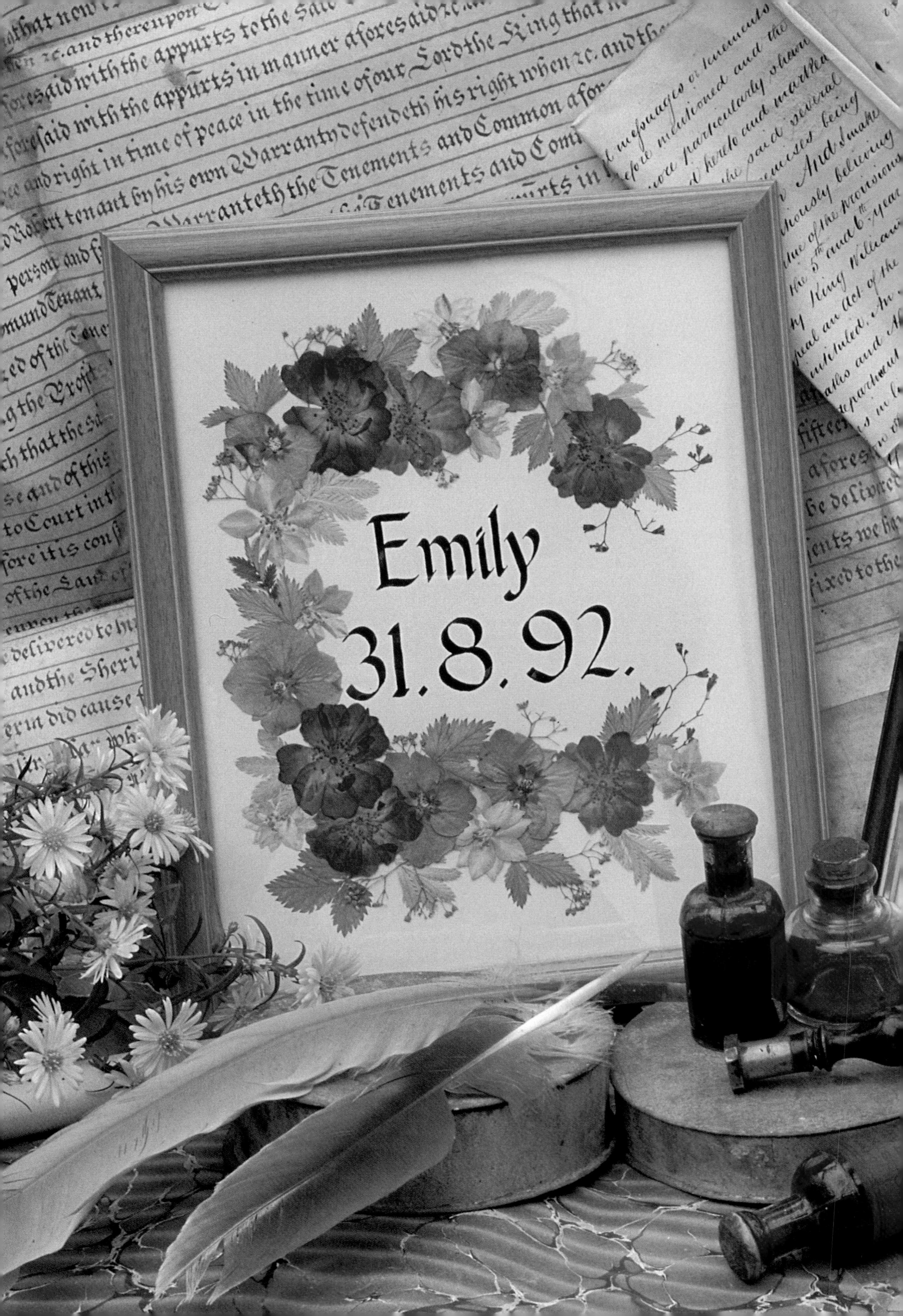
Emily
31.8.92.

Decorated calligraphy

Calligraphy is an art form that blends very well with pressed flowers. Whether you want to decorate a serious poem or an amusing saying, pressed flowers around the writing add to its attraction.

Gloria in excelsis Deo

$\mathscr{A}$ baby's birth date

Whether it's your own baby or that of a friend or relative, it is a lovely idea to commemorate the new celebration day by surrounding the baby's name and birth date with pressed flowers. The result is an unusual gift that can be hung in the nursery. If you choose, you might like to add other details, such as the baby's weight and length. This would be a charming gift to bring when you visit a new baby and mother in hospital, in which case you might like to use some of the flowers to make a matching card (see page 10).

INGREDIENTS

25cm × 20cm (10in × 8in) frame with glass cut to fit and a hardboard back (a photograph frame would be a suitable choice, as the background is card)

&

Cream or pale-coloured mount, to fit the frame, with the baby's name and date of birth either in calligraphy or formed with transfers

&

A selection of leaves and flowers

&

Latex adhesive

1 Start by positioning your chosen leaves to frame the calligraphy. Silverweed (Potentilla anserina) *and raspberry leaves, both of which have a lovely silvery-grey colouring, were used here.*

2 Next, add dainty touches of gypsophila and heuchera, and follow these with the large flowers, in this case the rose 'Yesterday', a hedging variety with semi-double flowers.

3 To finish, add some more flowers – pink larkspur and hydrangea florets, the latter with potentilla centres forming the middles. When you are happy with the design, secure each item with latex adhesive, applying it with a large needle. Cover the finished picture with clean glass and then fix it in the frame.

Gloria in excelsis

If you are not able to produce beautiful calligraphy – and it is an art form that requires practice – then try using a clear, copperplate style or just your ordinary handwriting. It is possible to buy special italic-style felt-tips from art shops, or you might find it easier to use transfers. Practise the spacing on scrap paper before using the cream card. You may find it helpful to make a sample on tracing paper and lay this over the card to check the effect.

INGREDIENTS

25cm × 20cm (10in × 8in) frame with glass cut to fit and a hardboard back (a photograph frame would be a suitable choice, as the background is card)

ಳಿ

Cream or pale-coloured mount, to fit the frame, with the chosen piece of calligraphy

ಳಿ

A selection of leaves and flowers

ಳಿ

Latex adhesive

1 Write your chosen text and then place some leaves around the writing. Blackberry leaves were used here, positioned upside down to show their beautiful grey undersides.

2 Having established the frame of the design with the larger leaves, begin to fill it out with some smaller ones. In this particular example, some small autumnal leaves and sprays of Alchemilla mollis *were used.*

3 Finish by positioning the larger flowers in the design. Here, cream Anemone japonica *were combined with some dark maroon pansies and a peach potentilla. The centres of the anemones are in fact spare potentilla middles. (When pressing flowers with fairly hard centres, it is easier to remove the centres and either press them separately or discard them and use a false centre, such as a centre from a potentilla or daisy, or a cow parsley floret.) When you are happy with the design, secure each item with adhesive, with a large needle. Cover the picture with clean glass and then fix it in the frame.*

Terracotta bowl
&
Garden posy

Pressed flower pictures can take many forms, and fresh arrangements can inspire a range of ideas. Two of these are shown here, and hopefully they may lead you to develop your own designs.

Terracotta bowl

Containers can be made from plant material, thin cardboard or fabric; this terracotta bowl is made from thin mount cardboard and looks very effective. Any colour can be used to make a vase of your choice; alternatively, you might use cotton fabric with a paisley or floral print to make a decorated vase. Beech leaves can give the effect of wood, while glass effects can be created with honesty seed pods.

INGREDIENTS

25cm × 20cm (10in × 8in) frame, and mount to fit, with large oval aperture

෨

Cream or white silk, slightly smaller than the mount, and 22.5cm × 17.5cm (9in × 7in) of foam, 12mm (½in) thick

෨

10cm × 15cm (4in × 6in) of thin terracotta-coloured cardboard

෨

Selection of leaves and flowers

෨

Narrow masking tape

෨

Latex adhesive

1 Prepare the mount and lay it over the hardboard and foam, as for the Spring picture (see step 1, page 24). Cut out a bowl shape from the terracotta mount card, drawing the shape on the back in pencil and then cutting it out with a craft knife.

2 Place the bowl on the mounted silk, and start positioning the leaves, in this case herb robert and raspberry. A small spray lying by the base of the bowl adds an extra touch of interest and helps to balance the picture.

3 Next, position the largest flowers. Anemone japonica have been used face-down here, as the underside of the petals has a pretty shimmer. With the anemones in place, some other small items – wormwood flowers and rue leaves – could be added.

4 Fill out the design with 'Ballerina' roses and potentillas ('Miss Willmot'), and then some more leaves. The spray at the bottom may lie to the right or left – the choice is yours. Fix the flowers and leaves in position, applying a little latex adhesive to the back of each with a large needle. Carefully clean the glass and place it on top of the picture. Place the frame in position and then turn the entire assembly upside down. The back can be secured with small panel pins placed at 2.5cm (1in) intervals, or with staples (use a framer's staple gun). Seal the back with masking tape.

Garden posy

This design features an informal posy, made with flowers that are easily grown in a small garden. A picture of a bridal bouquet could also be made in this style, and you might incorporate ribbons from the original bouquet, or perhaps a scrap of lace from the bride's dress. In a similar vein, you might preserve some flowers from a Mother's Day bouquet to make a picture of this type. To do this, you would have to remove some of the flowers for pressing while they were still at their peak, but the sacrifice would be worth making for a year-round reminder of a happy occasion.

INGREDIENTS

20cm × 15cm (8in × 6in) frame, with glass to fit and a hardboard back

❧

Mount to fit, with a large oval aperture

❧

White or cream silk, slightly smaller than the mount, and 17.5cm × 12.5cm (7in × 5in) of foam, 12mm (¹⁄₂in) thick

❧

Garden flowers and leaves, with some long stalks

❧

Narrow masking tape

❧

Latex adhesive

1 Prepare the mount and lay it over the hardboard and foam, as for the Spring picture (see step 1, page 24). Place the stalks in position and make a circle of leaves (in this case, raspberry and mugwort).

2 Add to the posy hydrangea florets, roses and larkspur, tucking the flowers so that they are not all piled on top of each other. Finish with smaller elements, such as forget-me-nots and small cream potentillas. Complete the picture as for the bowl (step 4, page 45).

Useful tips & Addresses

For details of courses, and for pressed flowers and components by post:

Joanna Sheen Limited
PO Box 52
Newton Abbot
Devon TQ12 4QH

For cards, stationery and film to cover pressed flowers:

Impress
Slough Farm
Westhall
Halesworth
Suffolk IP19 8RN

If you are new to the art of pressed flowers, you may wish to try growing some suitable flowers and leaves in your garden. The following small list of suggestions would form a very good basis for a pressed flower collection, but once you have successfully pressed some specimens then it is important to experiment with others, as this will inspire you to try out new design ideas.

Leaves Try pressing the new growth on rose bushes, some of which has a reddish tinge.

Many species of silver-leaved foliage prove useful to the pressed flower enthusiast, but the artemisia varieties 'Lambrook Silver' and 'Powys Castle' are particularly attractive.

Red, orange and brown autumnal leaves are worth pressing, especially those of the smaller shrubs – large leaves can be difficult to incorporate into designs for cards and other small items. The colour of red Japanese maple leaves keeps well after pressing.

Flowers Among seed packs, perhaps the best value for money would be a packet of mixed larkspur. The flowers include dark and pale pink, dark and pale blue, white and – very occasionally – some pretty lavender shades.

Small single roses can look very attractive in pictures. The 'Ballerina' rose and other patio types are worth considering.

Small white lawn daisies should not be ignored, particulary the first crop of the year, as this usually contains the largest flowers. Some daisies have a pink edge that is very pretty in designs.

Forget-me-nots are another easily-grown plant that will produce plenty of flowers for a modest outlay, and you will find that the petals keep their blue shade after pressing.

As can be seen from the designs in this book, potentillas are a good source of flowers, whether you choose a plant of the shrub variety or a herbaceous type such as 'Miss Willmott'.

To add dainty touches to your designs, there are several plants that will provide what might, for want of a better term, be called frilly bits. The Russian vine or mile-a-minute plant can be a nuisance to gardeners, but its creamy flowers press beautifully and look pretty in many different sizes of design. If you are growing sweet peas, then you will find that the flowers do not press very successfully, but the tendrils look wonderful. The common cow parsley often finds it way into the edges of the garden, and you will discover that it presses very well. Alternatively, you could press fennel flowers or a similar flower from the herb garden. A summer bedding flower that many gardeners find useful is alyssum. This also presses successfully, particularly the pink variety.